THE FLIGHTS OF ZARZA
ZARZA REMUEVE

Fernando Kofman
THE FLIGHTS OF ZARZA
Z A R Z A   R E M U E V E

∽

Translated by Ian Taylor
Introduced by Andrew Graham-Yooll

Published by Arc Publications,
Nanholme Mill, Shaw Wood Road
Todmorden OL14 6DA, UK

Original Spanish poems copyright © Fernando Kofman 2008
Translation copyright © Ian Taylor 2008
Introduction copyright © Andrew Graham-Yooll 2008

Design by Tony Ward
Printed by the MPG Book Group in the UK

978 1904614 37 1 (pbk)
978 1904614 90 6 (hbk)

ACKNOWLEDGEMENTS

Originally published in Argentina as *Zarza remueve* (Libros del Sicomoro, Buenos Aires 1992). Earlier versions of these translations appeared in the journals *Modern Poetry In Translation, Odyssey, Oxford Quarterly Review* and *STAND Magazine*.

Cover photograph: 'Ice' by Phoebe Ward

The publishers acknowledge financial assistance from
ACE Yorkshire

**Arc Publications: 'Visible Poets' series
Editor: Jean Boase-Beier**

CONTENTS

Series Editor's note / 7
Translator's preface / 9
Introduction / 13

La ciudad vacía / The Empty City

20 / Entrando en un mal sueño •	Entering a Bad Dream / 21
22 / Las olas del mar traen •	The Waves of the Sea / 23
24 / Zarza irrumpe •	Zarza Bursts In / 25
26 / Su ropa •	His Clothes / 27
28 / Cambios en la Catedral •	Changes in the Cathedral / 29
30 / Las bodas que cierran septiembre •	The Wedding that Closes September / 31

Atracción del Norte / The Attraction of the North

34 / El camino hacia Posadas •	The Road to Posadas / 35
36 / Posadas como Johannesburgo •	Posadas as Johannesburg / 37
38 / Los maizales cibernéticos •	The Cybernetic Maize Fields / 39
40 / Zarza-dama del aserradero •	Zarza-Donna of the Sawmill / 41
42 / Un parque de diversiones en Apóstoles •	An Amusement Park in Apostles / 43
44 / Zarza-mestizo •	Zarza-Mestizo / 45
46 / Cuerpos abandonados •	Abandoned Bodies / 47
48 / Encuentro con la voz •	Encounter with the Voice / 49
52 / Trucos de la voz interior •	Deceits of the Interior Voice / 53

Derrumbe en el Sur / Precipice in the South

56 / Un extenso país •	A Vast Country / 57
58 / La lavandera mapuche •	The Mapuche Washergirl / 59
60 / Ante el impostor •	In the Presence of the Impostor / 61
62 / Espiando a los escolares •	Observing the Schoolchildren / 63
64 / La granja-Comunidad •	The Farm-Community / 65

66 / Carta desde el manicomio • Letter from the Mental Hospital / 67
68 / De pronto recibimos una conciencia • All at Once we Receive Another's Consciousness / 69

Después de la muerte, recomienzo / After death, I begin again

72 / Después de la muerte, recomienzo • After Death, I Begin Again / 73
74 / Para terminar con la pareja • To be Done with the Couple / 75
76 / La televisión multiplica siempre • Television Multiplying into Infinity / 77
78 / Bar "Trelew" • "Trelew" Bar / 79
82 / El Chubut deja su historia de la amistad • The Chubut Bequeaths its History of Friendship / 83
86 / Para la memoria no hay olvido • For Memory there is No Oblivion / 87
88 / Antes de unirnos, en Gaiman • Before we Come Together, in Gaiman / 89
90 / Es la extraña noche que nos desnuda • It is the Strange Night that Undresses Us / 91

Biographical Notes / 93

SERIES EDITOR'S NOTE

There is a prevailing view of translated poetry, especially in England, which maintains that it should read as though it had originally been written in English. The books in the 'Visible Poets' series aim to challenge that view. They assume that the reader of poetry is by definition someone who wants to experience the strange, the unusual, the new, the foreign, someone who delights in the stretching and distortion of language which makes any poetry, translated or not, alive and distinctive. The translators of the poets in this series aim not to hide but to reveal the original, to make it visible and, in so doing, to render visible the translator's task too. The reader is invited not only to experience the unique fusion of the creative talents of poet and translator embodied in the English poems in these collections, but also to speculate on the processes of their creation and so to gain a deeper understanding and enjoyment of both original and translated poems.

Jean Boase-Beier

TRANSLATOR'S PREFACE

I was given a copy of Fernando Kofman's *Zarza remueve* at the start of a five-month stay in Buenos Aires over ten years ago, and was immediately enchanted by the clarity of the language and solidity of the imagery, and also had the great pleasure of getting to know Kofman as a person. His spoken Spanish is exactly the same as his written; in contrast to the quick, often indistinct rush of words spoken by most *porteños*, Kofman – born in the province of Misiones, which he left for Buenos Aires at the age of 20 – speaks a far slower, crystal-clear Spanish. For me his way of speaking perfectly mirrors his character, that of a patient man with a nevertheless urgent need to communicate with as little obfuscation as possible with everyone he meets or who reads his work, but to whom clarity does not imply dullness, what he most urgently wants to communicate being that which constantly eludes communication: all the beauty and mystery, the images and truths whose impossible expression will forever be the main mission of poetry.

The first poem I read, and instantly decided to translate, was 'A Vast Country' (pp. 56 / 7) – seeing similarities in it with some of my own poetry, I was naïve enough to think I already knew the writer inside out, knew the philosophy behind his writings and the style to which he would adhere in order to get that philosophy across, and thought he would be easy to translate. Quickly scanning through a few more of the poems I thought I was right: here was a writer whose poetry tended wholly towards narrative prose and I would have no problems. As I read more closely, however, I realised how wrong I was. Kofman is a very 'slippery' writer, the general 'prose' feeling being offset by healthy portions of the abstract, ungraspable meanings, and the occasional roughness of language. Such elements are discussed in his book of short essays, *La cultura depende del lenguaje* ('Culture depends on language'), in which he writes of his preference for artists interested in falling through the 'cracks' in language: Joyce, Kafka, Robbe-Grillet, Beckett, Butor and so on, writers who seek to disrupt the normal communicative mode of writing, celebrating the difficult above the easy, allowing the reader more creativity in unravelling the work's meanings. Kofman can in no way – and nor would he wish to – be compared with such writers, his poetry having a more mainstream lean, but he has taken many tips from them that allow him to disrupt the 'mainstream' surface, all of which create stumbling blocks for what would otherwise be an easy translation task.

People often speak of the "Anglicised Spanish" of Jorge Luis Borges, the way his use of words, his syntax, punctuation *et al* mirrored the English language. Though Kofman lists Borges among his influences and has been touched with the linguistic clarity of the latter, his own language remains totally Argentinian, whether in subject matter, attitude, choice of words or punctuation. The punctuation was the more interesting, and occasionally problematic, aspect of the translation, especially where commas are used in a way that, in English, would be seen as an unnecessary way of breaking up the flow of a sentence: a comma separating the subject from the rest of the sentence. This occurs, for example, in 'The Wedding that Closes September' (pp. 30 / 1 ("pone su bisagra, entre octubre y septiembre" – *places its hinge between October and September*) and 'In the Presence of the Impostor' (pp. 60 / 1) ("ella-Zarza, no detuvo su canto" – *she-Zarza did not stop her singing*). 'The Wedding that closes September' includes another curious use of commas, the final verse being peppered with them in a way that, for me, seems to imitate the pauses of someone fighting against laughter when telling an anecdote – an irritating person, obviously, as Kofman himself finds the anecdote totally unfunny. It would have looked too odd to transfer such punctuation into English and so I have attempted to mirror the choppy effect produced with commas in the original with short sharp lines.

I also feel that he sometimes uses commas for another, more deliberate reason. At readings Kofman recites his poems at a slow, reflective pace, and I feel he uses punctuation almost as guidelines regarding the pace at which he intends his works to be read. Repeating this in English would look extremely artificial, so I can only hope that readers recognise at what pace a poem is best read without such markings.

What struck me at several points in the translation is the concision with which Spanish-language authors are able to express themselves compared with their English-language counterparts, an example of which occurred in the poem 'El Chubut deja su historia de la amistad' ('The Chubut Bequeaths its History of Friendship', pp. 82 / 3):

> Cuando el puño de uno
> va a caer sobre el rostro del otro,
> viene el policía, habla con los dos
> y me mira.

This is a curious instance because whereas I can literally translate the first two lines and find they perfectly mirror the semi-colloquial, witty English that would be used to describe the situation – "Just as the fist of one / is about to fall on the face of the other" – the following two lines, if translated literally, would be deeply inexpressive in their minimalism: "the policeman comes, speaks with the two / and looks at me". Therefore I expanded upon them in keeping with the character of the first two lines: "a policeman turns up, asks what's going on / and throws the odd glance in my direction".

I nevertheless feel that the 'difficulties' mentioned above are extremely slight, if not altogether irrelevant, for on the whole *The Flights of Zarza* was a relatively easy, enjoyable translation experience. Such is the general clarity, and easy 'transferability', of Kofman's language that it was almost impossible for the translation *not* to be extremely faithful, indeed at times an almost *literal* translation, allowing me to be faithful to the original without falling into slavish dullness. I also enjoyed the occasional 'translation miracle', as for instance in 'The Waves of the Sea' (p. 22 / 23) when, while translating faithfully and without artifice, the last seven lines formed a pattern that coincided with the sinking / shrinking-downward tone of those lines. This was just one pleasure among many, and I can only hope that my translation is effective enough for readers to experience their own pleasure from this first English-language encounter with Fernando Kofman.

Ian Taylor

INTRODUCTION

The poetry of Argentina of the Nineties should have an influence on the art of creation well into the twenty-first century. The phenomenon, the influence, must be seen as part of the poetry of Latin America as a whole. The emergence from dictatorship and ferocious repression in the Seventies and Eighties freed the language in the Nineties, in greater or lesser degree, from the River Plate to Central America.

Fernando Kofman offers an early reflection of this trend in a short essay in the sixth (and last) issue of his magazine *Satura*,[1] printed in 1984, just as democratic rule returned to Argentina after seven years of state terror. Given his own strong Jewish background, he compared Argentina's dictatorship with Germany under the Nazis and echoed George Steiner in the remark that "language was not innocent of the horror".[2] The circumstance of literature in those times, wrote Kofman in *Satura*, "had its similarities with what happened in Germany, despite a number of differences. Some poets chose to write and not publish, their creation was mutilated at all times by the ever-present threat of death and an awareness of the nonsense of attempting to publish in a time ruled by crime and propaganda... But the need for expression remained and led to the establishment of those small windows that were the little magazines, which permitted the circulation of views and ideas in a limited circle... These windows were brief illusions in a prospect of ruins. Other poets developed the practice of forgetting."

Poetry in Argentina had to shake itself free of such a stranglehold. Throughout Latin America, poetry has always been inseparable from the time of the poet, even if some poets wrote to be read after death. Jorge Luis Borges (1899-1986) might have disputed this view. He managed to keep his political views firmly out of his

---

[1] Kofman is currently editor of the magazine *Frank Baires*, which develops writing on ideas from the School of Frankfurt in Buenos Aires. Its first issue was printed in June 2005. He has also published in the Argentine magazines *Omero, El Jabalí, Diario de Poesía, Hablar de Poesía* and *Barataria*.
[2] See also, *A Lexicon of Terror, Argentina and the Legacies of Torture*, by Marguerite Feitlowitz (OUP, 1998).

writing. Nonetheless, his translator Norman Thomas di Giovanni (b. 1933) detects the politics in Borges even while he tried to put himself above or apart from the turmoil of his many decades.

There is probably a bit of Borges in every Argentine poet, and by extension in all South American poets, but at the same time they are also the children of Chileans Pablo Neruda (1904-73) and Nicanor Parra (b. 1914), the Mexican Octavio Paz (1914-98), the Nicaraguan Ruben Darío (1867-1916), or the Brazilian Carlos Drummond de Andrade (1902-87). In Latin America, poetry and the time in which it is produced have an intense relationship, comparable perhaps only with the Russians of the first half of the twentieth century.

Fernando Kofman was born in 1947, in Posadas, capital of the subtropical province of Misiones, that short stretch of Argentina that jabs into the southeastern corner of Brazil. In 1967, he moved south to Buenos Aires and has lived in different parts of the city and its suburbs until he has made them all home. Since then he has written poetry, short essays, and a handful of plays, publishing on the fringe, in small magazines, until his first book, *Ten Poems and a Contribution*,[3] appeared in 1979. This last date and his age do not make Kofman a member of the Nineties generation, but like others who came through the dictatorship, either in the silence of those who stayed in Argentina or in the stridence of those who went into exile, it was in the Eighties and early Nineties that artists in Argentina found a new voice.

Three of Kofman's books, including *The Flights of Zarza* (1992), were published in that decade of unabashed consumerism. This was a period when the Argentina of the Washington Consensus (1989),

---

[3] Fernando Kofman has published six books of poetry: *Diez poemas y un aporte* (Ten Poems and one Contribution), (1979), *Tiempo de convulsion* (Time of Convulsion), (1982), *Caída de la catedral* (Fall from the Cathedral), (1987), *Zarza remueve* (Flights of Zarza), (1992), *De Bell a Campana* (From Bell to Campana), (1995) and *El dúo de música de cámara* (The Chamber Music Duo), (2001). And he has published five books of short essays: *Poesía entre dos épocas* (Poetry between Two Ages), (1985), *Polifonía en el páramo* (Polyphony in the Wasteland), (1990), *La cultura depende del lenguaje* (Culture depends on Language), (1997), *Poesía para la arquitectura* (Poetry for Architecture), (2000), *La insolación* (Sunstroke), (2004).

then madly racing to counter the hyper-inflation of the Eighties that followed the dictatorship, became a "wanna-be" US shopping mall. In such an environment, and as more and more publishing houses became appendages of vast international commercial groups, poetry became what the poet Edgardo Dobry (b. 1962) described as, "the last refuge of internal life, the scene of singularity and individuality". It was no longer just an escape from military repression but was a place of refuge for the literary language of a whole society. This is what Kofman captures in his writing. Inspired by Theodor Adorno (1903-69) – in spite of the latter's view in 1949 that "To write a poem after Auschwitz is an act of barbarism" – Kofman sees a time for a renewal of voices. What Adorno saw as the drop of a curtain, Kofman interprets as a signal that there was no going back in the language of creation, because Auschwitz had changed everything. After the horror, the rebirth.

From that point of departure, Kofman's writing grows out of the broadness of his reading, which embraces a vast worldly range and prompts him to write in *Polyphony in the Wasteland* (1990), "Now I know that I could not emigrate". That short statement contains the development of a sense of place for his poetry and a conflict in the growth of his writing. It expresses a great divide between the past and the need to move on, the break of the poetry of the Nineties with the politics of the Seventies, which plagued every line of writing of those years. A new language was expanded from the old and thereby became a reservoir for the change still needed. Kofman is clear that he belongs to Buenos Aires, where an urban poetry was created in the 1920s, with the city as the main protagonist. It was a poetry unknown to any other city in the world, and Kofman is convinced about this belonging in his text.

Scenes of Buenos Aires, the magnet for European sensibility in the constant search for a meaning to Argentina, the meaning of a European city in a flat empty space called the pampa, pepper Kofman's writing. The product has been ably "transferred", not just translated, by English poet Ian Taylor, who follows the androgynous character of the title, Zarza, to northern Argentina and then south, always with Buenos Aires as the centre of the circle.

Daniel Samoilovich (b. 1949), in the introduction to the bilingual anthology *Twenty Poets from Argentina* (Redbeck Press, 2004), offers the view that poetry in Argentina, and elsewhere in the continent, in the Nineties had a "richness [that] is in part nurtured by the three preceding decades but the passage of time has generated new frontiers, influences, crossed readings: poor is the poet who stuck to the lines of a trend without contributing a personal content, the re-evaluation of what was read and admired, or even in that previously written by him."

Argentine poet and critic Vicente Muleiro (b. 1951) has written that in the poetry of the Nineties "The relation between text and context is more palpable than in other periods because it no longer uses any subterfuge to elude issues." (*Clarín*, 24 December 2005).

In a more sceptical attitude, poet and critic Daniel Freidemberg (b. 1945) has said that "Sometimes it [the poetry of the Nineties] works, and sometimes – often – nothing happens, but in any case we will have to see, when it does work, how it works: as a simple entertainment, as an occasion on which to appreciate the audacity and art of the author, or as an experience in which the reader stops being what he / she is and changes his / her relationship with language and the world, at least for a short while." (*Clarín*, 24 December 2005).

More politically, Argentine academic and critic Jorge Monteleone (b. 1957) is straightforward in his appraisal of the poets of the Nineties. "The Argentine poets of the last two decades have struggled with an extreme situation in history: the reconstruction of the social language which had been contaminated by the repressive discourse of the military dictatorship. Not only have they achieved this, but they have also restored in their fashion the paradox of the poem: they recovered the social narrative from the furiously individual, the new ways of seeing, the intimate experiences" (*Clarín*, 24 December 2005).

Kofman fits comfortably into this context, and Ian Taylor has done well to introduce him to an English readership.

Andrew Graham-Yooll

THE FLIGHTS OF ZARZA
ZARZA REMUEVE

THE EMPTY CITY
LA CIUDAD VACÍA

ENTRANDO EN UN MAL SUEÑO

Entrando en un mal sueño
veo a los sauces murmurar,
los malvones crisparse, el grillo en silencio,
la voz del río cercano
deambular entre piedras, gaviotas, caña,
hacia el vientre sucio del océano.

Este torbellino que cruza mi ventana
mezcla de sueño, vigilia, opiniones,
la historia narrada por Dalí,
demente vendaval que entra en mis ojos,
es detenido, transformado por mi cerebro.

El reloj marca las tres. Creo ver
que la historia en Gaiman se detiene,
el tiempo navega entre mares invisibles,
el grillo, oscuro bulto detrás de mi ventana,
muestra su precaria entereza.
En esta hora quisiera afirmar
que la historia se detiene,
las pesadillas simulan que han partido
escasos segundos, un parpadeo,
hasta que un gran sueño las reclama.

ENTERING A BAD DREAM

Entering a bad dream
I see the willows whisper,
the geraniums tense, the cricket sit in silence,
while the voice of the nearby river
meanders among stones, gulls and reeds
towards the ocean's filthy gut.

This whirlwind raging outside my window
merges sleep, wakefulness, opinions,
history according to Salvador Dalí;
a demented gale that penetrates my eyes,
and then comes to a stop,
transformed by my brain.

The clock says three. I have the feeling
that history has stopped in Gaiman,
time navigates between invisible seas;
the cricket, a vague, immobile form at the window,
displays its precarious fortitude.
At this hour I would like to declare
that history has stopped,
the nightmares pretend to have gone on their way –
a few seconds tick by, the blink of an eye,
before an enormous dream claims them.

LAS OLAS DEL MAR TRAEN

Las olas del mar traen
cuerpos sin ojos, mitades de cerebro,
manos y muslos dispersos,
caballeras entretejidas con algas,
volúmenes de carne bajo periódicos:
"la nueva navaja", "Irak avanza",
fragmentos recortados por un faro
entre la sal de las dunas y las rocas.

Cuerpos que suben y bajan
del mar a la tierra, de tierra al mar
y la tormenta que en la noche amenaza
dejar a oscuras el delgado faro.
Todo parece acostumbrado descenso
o vieja destrucción
para un momento que se repite
en el vientre del mar, en la pulpa de los periódicos,
acción violenta que nos visita
cruzando la luz y la sombra,
y que una boya marina – nosotros –
vigila como noticia normal,
desde la playa oscura.

THE WAVES OF THE SEA

The waves of the sea bring
eyeless corpses, brains ripped in half,
severed hands and thighs,
locks of hair entangled with weed,
pieces of flesh wrapped in newspaper
– "A NEW KIND OF RAZOR",
"IRAQ ADVANCES" –
fragments caught in the glare of a lighthouse
amid the salt of the dunes and the rocks.

Corpses that ebb and flow
from sea to land, land to sea,
and the storm that in the night threatens
to throw the thin lighthouse into darkness.
All seems resigned to sad descent
or age-old destructiveness,
caught in that moment forever repeating itself
in the belly of the sea, the newspapers' pulp;
violent action that comes to pay us a visit,
crossing through light and shadow,
and which a buoy – ourselves –
observes as normal news
from the dark beach.

ZARZA IRRUMPE

Me asomé al puente y respondió: el vacío
vigilé la escollera y murmuró: el vacío
desde el bote desfondado, las flores
muertas, lanzaron un sonido que me atrajo:
vacío, vacío.

Y de la tierra negra se escaparon risas
como los ojos deformes de un tabernero,
en cada rincón donde la brisa crujía
hablaba el vacío.

Pero un cuerpo disuelto trajo su vocecita
era la bruma con cabello rojo
rostro difuso y huellas invisibles,
tintineante luz sacudida por viento,
y el vacío se fue.

ZARZA BURSTS IN

I looked out from the bridge and *it* responded:
emptiness
as I watched the breakwater I heard its murmurs:
emptiness
from the broken boat and the dead flowers
there came a sound that bewitched me:
emptiness
emptiness

And laughter came cackling out of the black earth
like the deformed eyes of a publican,
in every corner where the breeze creaked
spoke the emptiness.

But the faint voice of a dissolved body
could also be heard –
it was the red-haired mist,
a vague face, invisible footprints,
the jangling of a lantern shaken by the wind,
and the emptiness went away.

SU ROPA

Su cuerpo se resiste a entrar
en bellas camisas, impermeables
elegantes. Rechaza la brisa fresca
de un perfume. Sus ojos no
destellan. Hay dolor.

El frío lo encuentra
con lo que tiene, campera y bufanda,
mirada distante para
el desfile repetido:
ropa magnífica entre escombros.

Está el calor de sus manos
suavemente llevadas a su boca,
el rostro se ilumina como una brasa.
Todo él es caldeado aliento. Pero otra
luz empobrece este calor,
los reflectores de una gran tienda.

Ante su mesa el vino
se dilata. No por milagro sí
por goce. La sopa y la longaniza vuelcan
rápidas satisfacciones, en eso que es
un estómago. No deseando más,
hundido en la cama,
escucha lo que su ropa dice,
comentario modesto que niega
su sueño,
donde es figura ostentosa.

HIS CLOTHES

His body was not made
for beautiful shirts
or elegant raincoats.
He has no nose for the fresh
breeze of a perfume. The sparkle has long
gone out of his eyes,
where there is now only pain.

    He faces the cold with whatever
he happens to be wearing,
an old jacket, a woollen scarf,
his gaze never registering
the endless fashion parade,
luxurious clothes amid the rubble.

    The warmth of his hands
gently raised to his mouth
makes his face glow like ember
heated by his own breath. But this warmth
is offset by another light,
the neon glare of a giant department store.

    At his table the wine
lasts forever. Not by miracle
but sheer savouring.
The soup and spicy sausage flood satisfaction
into the pit of his stomach. Sated, contented,
sunken into his bed, he is painfully aware
of what his clothes have to say,
a humble story belying his dreams
of being the world's most elegant dandy.

CAMBIOS EN LA CATEDRAL

La piedra recibe la débil luz,
gris mañana que desfila entre los sauces,
flota en el pasto, se disuelve en la niebla,
por ratos muestra la mole simétrica:
Catedral de La Plata sobre un manto verde.

Voy hacia ella y recorro su interior,
un eco de madera, mármoles, resignación,
me reciben. Al fondo, la silueta de Zarza
se aleja, las paredes interpretan
sus gemidos,
red de palabras y agudos silencios.

La tarde me muestra cambios imprevistos,
no una arquitectura que canta
sino una vacía Estación Terminal;
(¿Fue Zarza quien produjo este hecho
de revelar la cara mercantil de la piedra?)

y la piedra se ofrece oscura
y la tarde se ofrece oscura.

CHANGES IN THE CATHEDRAL

The stone receives the weak light
of a grey morning that slowly drifts among the willows,
floats on the meadow, dissolves in the mist,
revealing bit by bit the vast symmetry
of Plate Cathedral on a green mantle.

I walk inside and look around,
am greeted by an echo
of wood, marble and resignation.
In the background the shadow of Zarza
withdraws, leaving his groans to find
their expression in the walls –
a web of words and intense silences.

The afternoon brings unexpected changes,
no longer an architecture that sings
but a deserted terminal station
(Was Zarza the one behind this event,
exposing the true, commercial face of the stone?)

and the stone offers darkness,
the afternoon offers darkness.

LAS BODAS QUE CIERRAN SEPTIEMBRE

    Descubro a los novios sonrientes,
bailar con el padrino rojo como un gallo,
apretado en su smoking, y el novio
zarandeado y volando por el aire,
entre los brazos y rostros cómplices.
So las muestras de una casa de fotos,
ofreciendo hasta el cansancio el mismo caso
    la unión y la promesa repetida
    que no se quebrará hasta la gran bronca.

    Las mismas parejas que se me cruzan
son el anuncio de imprevisibles uniones,
remando por el Tigre o montados en sus bicis,
alegremente hablando en los bosques de Palermo,
en ese instante en que el año nuevo judío
    se abre, pone su bisagra,
    entre octubre y septiembre.
Ofrecen toda su energía sexual
como aquella que derraman los troncos
    sobre la tierra.

    Nada puede reemplazar a la vieja foto
detenido en un tiempo irreal – la boda –
ni darle otra condición: un tiempo
que se modela según sus protagonistas.
    La torta del aniversario
o la cena del aniversario,
tienen la mansedumbre del Delta,
o de la anécdota chispeante,
siempre bien elegida,
de cuando el novio meó exigido
detrás de los árboles del parque,
apenas, un segundo después,
de que el cura o el rabino
    le diera una esposa.

THE WEDDING THAT CLOSES SEPTEMBER

     I see the beaming newlyweds
dancing with the best man (rooster-red face
protruding from a tuxedo many sizes too small),
the swaggering groom flying through the air,
flanked by the arms and faces of accomplices.
Just one sample among many in the photo-shop,
the same event displayed *ad nauseam*:
     the union, the eternally repeated promise
     never to be broken
     until the great row do us part.

     Every couple that passes by me
declares the wonder of unforeseeable unions,
as they row along the Tigre, glide by on their bikes,
chattering and kissing in the woods of Palermo,
in that moment when the Jewish New Year begins,
     swinging open on its hinge
     between September and October.
They offer all their sexual energy
like the sap of a tree
     scattered onto the soil.

     Nothing can replace an old photograph
capturing one split-second of unreal wedding time,
nor alter it in any way, this time
shaped irretrievably by its protagonists.
     The anniversary cake
     or the anniversary dinner
are as lifeless as the Delta,
as insipid as the endlessly
repeated witty anecdote,
about the groom pissing in desperation
behind some bushes in the park
within the blink of an eye
of the priest or rabbi
     presenting him with a wife.

THE ATTRACTION OF THE NORTH
ATRACCIÓN DEL NORTE

EL CAMINO HACIA POSADAS

La lluvia terminó, las aguas yacen oscuras
por el movimiento de la tormenta
que sacude al granero, a los pocos árboles,
al borde de la ruta. Este presente
demasiado ágil, tiene por mi memoria
la condición de regreso al pasado
en sube y baja, incesante,
como cada colina inundada.

¿Cómo me mira ese buey, con el agua hasta
el cuello; mira al adolescente que creció
vanidoso, satisfecho de sus fuerzas, lanzando
una mirada hiriente sobre el mundo?

¿Y la campana de la capilla de madera
agitada por un chico mutilado,
de qué modo me trae los arroyos,
la violación de la joven por la pandilla salvaje?

El agua consume todo tiempo,
disuelve la memoria en su movimiento.
Pasado está bajo esas negras pezuñas,
futuro en la lectura en penumbras del mutilado,
y presente, en esta carretera, bordeada por aguas,
coronada de oscuridad, cruzada
por los miedos de los que viajan,
grandes miedos
nacidos de pequeños y mezquinos miedos.

THE ROAD TO POSADAS

The rain now stopped, the puddles lie dark and ruffled
beneath the violence of the storm
as it shakes the granary, the few trees
at the side of the road. This flexible present taps into
my memory, into the depths of the past,
sinking and re-surfacing
like hills above floodwater.

How does this ox see me as he stands
with the water up to his neck?
Does he see the adolescent growing vain,
over-confident, his features distorted as he casts
a wounding glance at the world?

And the bell in the wooden chapel
rung by a crippled boy,
how exactly does it bring back to me
that stream where a gang of savages
stole a young girl's innocence?

The water consumes all time,
dissolves memory in its movement.
It is the past beneath those black hooves,
the future in the crippled boy's penumbral reading,
and the present in this road bordered by waters,
crowned with darkness, crossed by the fears
of every traveller,
overwhelming fears
born from those once small and petty.

POSADAS COMO JOHANNESBURGO

Está la fría mente calculando
cómo evitará toda acción,
están las manos rústicas y sometidas
cepillando la misma madera,
son sucesos donde la acción y
la meditación van separados
como las partes de un cuerpo dividido,
pero esto te conforma ¿es tu propósito?
sumar días y días a esta disociación.

Como la extraña silueta de las palmeras
brotando de los alrededores de Posadas,
había sucesos para la acción: una
acción paralizante, un cuerpo negro volcado
sobre la tierra, atendiendo sus mandiocas,
y sucesos para fijar la meditación,
el futuro profesor especulando con algunos datos;
situaciones y hechos que rechazaban una unión,
la que lleva de la mente a las manos,
de la meditación a la acción
de la oscuridad a la luz, y viceversa.

POSADAS AS JOHANNESBURG

It is the cold mind calculating
how to avoid all action,
it is the rustic, subject hands
forever planing the same bit of wood:
all these events where action and meditation
exist separately like the two halves
of a divided body.
Is this really how you want it to be,
how you have chosen to live your life,
each day splitting you further and further apart?

Like the strange shadows of the palm trees
rising up around Posadas,
there were events that called for action,
a paralysing action, the body of a black man
knocked to the ground while tending his cassavas;
and events for meditation:
the future teacher quietly wondering
what certain facts could mean:
situations and events that never cohere,
never enabling the mind to act through the hands,
to turn thought into action,
darkness into light
and vice versa.

LOS MAIZALES CIBERNÉTICOS

Zarza despertó en un extenso maizal.

Eran columnas, gajos multicolores,
del tamaño de un pino, con el peso
de un pino.

Quedó descontrolado por sus energías,
marejadas de ululantes voces vegetales
      que acechaban a cada hombre,
los dejaban entrar y consumían sus hígados,
caían sobre sus cuerpos y luego se alzaban
exhibiendo huesos, cráneos, brazos,
      junto a sus raíces.

Una endemoniada arquitectura
había surgido.

Los maizales cloqueaban cada muerte.

Alejándose,
      Zarza se arrodilló y miró.

THE CYBERNETIC MAIZE FIELDS

Zarza awoke in an enormous maize field.

There were columns and cuttings of every colour,
each as high and as dense
as a pine tree.

Their energies sapped Zarza of all control,
waves of howling vegetable voices
      lying in wait for every man,
enticing them in and then devouring their livers,
falling on their bodies then lifting them up in the air,
displaying bones, skulls, arms
      along with their roots.

A demonic architecture
had arisen.

The maize fields applauded each death.

Withdrawing,
      Zarza knelt down and watched.

ZARZA-DAMA DEL ASERRADERO

El humo me lanza hacia atrás
cuando tenía carita de monja,
labios diminutos y su cuerpo jadeaba
sobre mí, en el auto, olvidándose
del afuera, entre los naranjos, donde
el negro ardía en su choza.

Los pinos chamuscados,
el vivero como lonja de ceniza, los
cerdos huyendo hacia el monte,
se instalan cíclicamente en mis ojos
      mediante una lágrima.
Ahora, él llega del aserradero,
paga a los peones, bromea con ellos.
Nuevo humo me trae nuevas lágrimas.
Nuevos incendios agigantan más rostros
lívidos, espantados ante las llamas,
como yo aquella noche,
bajo su peso satisfecho, exhausto.

ZARZA-DONNA OF THE SAWMILL

The smoke throws me back
to her sweet little face like a nun's,
her tiny lips, her body panting
on top of me in the car, oblivious
to what was happening outside,
the black man burning to death
in his shack among the orange trees.

      The pine trees scorched, the nursery reduced
to a scattering of ash, the pigs squealing
as they ran to the hills:
these images come and go
      fixed by a tear in my eyes.

And now the boss comes out of the sawmill,
pays the workers, cracks a few jokes.
New smoke brings me new tears.
New fires enlarge more faces,
pale with terror before the flames,
just as I was that night
as I lay beneath her body,
satisfied, exhausted.

UN PARQUE DE DIVERSIONES EN APÓSTOLES

La "vuelta al mundo" lo elevó hasta un cielo,
precario cielo donde recibió la lluvia,
y luego vino el palacio de espejos, el lanzador
de cuchillos, la taza giratoria,
un mestizo que soplaba fuego ante sus ojos.
Sobre el carro-teatrito, una marioneta que era su réplica,
luchaba con un verdugo, un predicador, un músico.
El viento y la lluvia no cedían, entrando y danzando,
en la carne de los pocos que miraban.

Zarza no quiso ver el final.
Al irse escuchó:
una música horrible, un breve festejo con carcajadas.
Mojado, se cruzó con mis ojos,
mientras un altavoz recitaba

publicidades, fragmentos de Mateo.

AN AMUSEMENT PARK IN APOSTLES

The Ferris Wheel carried him up to heaven,
a precarious heaven where he was drenched by the rain.
And then the hall of mirrors appeared, the knife
thrower, the spinning cup,
a mestizo blowing smoke before his eyes.
On the theatrical float a puppet carved in his image
fought with a tyrant, a preacher, a musician.
The wind and rain drove on relentlessly,
a wild jig dancing beneath the skin
of the few spectators.

Zarza didn't want to see how it ended.
As he left he heard a burst of terrible music,
roars of laughter, the general sounds of celebration.
Soaked to the skin, he passed before me,
while voices droned out of a loudspeaker:

messages from our sponsors,
fragments from the book of Matthew.

ZARZA-MESTIZO

Cayó cuando el agua tocaba
sus tobillos.
Ninguna campana lo anunciaba
lo detenía en su descenso.
Solo,
su rostro de guaraní anciano
ante aquellas residencias
reteniendo una visión:
      el podrido tonel
que alimenta a pocos insectos.

      Un surco de noche vacía
aclaró sus ideas
– guaraní – educación – lecturas
islas remotas – se dijo,
 a las que no lleva
ningún puente.

ZARZA-MESTIZO

When the water was up to his ankles
he fell.
No bell announced him
nor stopped him in his descent.
Alone,
with his ancient Guarani face
clashing with those houses,
he recalled a vision:
      the rotten barrel
eaten by insects.

      A stretch of empty night
clarified his thoughts:
Guarani… education… readings…
remote islands
– he said to himself –
      to which he'll never find a bridge

CUERPOS ABANDONADOS

No podés evadirte de la mutilación
sobre los cuerpos abandonados en los charcos,
trabajo del verdugo alentado por muchos,
de la navaja sigilosa, de la descarga eléctrica;
música que brota mientras el tren
parece cruzar las historias.

Bajo el terraplén, en el barro, los de la ambulancia
examinen: ¿suicida, vagabundo, ejecutado o "prófugo"?
Un cuerpo joven que las ruedas seccionaron.
Toda una hora para vaciar la cerveza
o el café, "emocionarse" desde el vagón-comedor,
con la parábola-ilusión de Corazón Aquino,
la historia redimida por fe
(no sometida a locura y sangre).

Un canto enfático intenta el titular
de ese diario doblado, cubierto por la noche
y las risas, o los comentarios displicentes
del vagón, atendiendo la sola música
de sus labios. Cerca de Chajarí quedó
ese bulto, puesto por los hechos en nuestra mesa,
y por nosotros, rápidamente consagrado,
como olvidable reliquia.

ABANDONED BODIES

There's no escaping the mutilations inflicted
upon the bodies abandoned in the puddles,
the work of the executioner cheered on by thousands;
the concealed switchblade, the electrical charge;
music that rises while the train
seems to cross histories.

Below the embankment, in the mud, the paramedics
look for clues: suicide, vagabond, hit, "refugee"…?
A young body cut to pieces by the wheels.
An hour's journey to spend drinking beer or coffee,
getting worked up, "moved to tears",
in the dining car
over the illusion of history redeemed by faith,
no longer at the mercy of madness and blood,
as told in the parable of Corazón Aquino.

The headline sings its shrill song from the folded newspaper
obscured by the night and the laughter
and blasé remarks of the commuters,
the only music these people hear
being the sound of their own voices. It was near Chajarí
that this object was found, before being brought
to our tables by the crime section,
and then instantly filed away
as a forgettable relic.

ENCUENTRO CON LA VOZ

Para Navidad recuento mis años
momentos oscuros metidos en los huesos
vigilándome en un andén, tirando un boleto,
saliendo o entrando entre molinetes;
viajando por un canal de voces
que me arrastran a ningún sitio.

Resguardado por la estación abovedada
mi cuerpo deslizándose busca un punto,
un refugio de silencio y mínima reflexión
donde las vehemencias se examinen.
Encuentra en su camino pensamientos cansados,
instalados en rostros cansados.

Sin órgano ni Biblia, acompañado por mi mujer,
la cama, una mesita, la medianoche,
no veo mi pieza (iluminada por una débil lámpara)
como sitio para mi voz interior,
mientras ella explora mis momentos,
remueve indecisa mis limitaciones.

En la mañana, con un pequeño ojo abierto
sobre el cielo nublado, revuelvo el café,
mastico las medialunas, hojeo rápido el "Clarín"
que hace ostentación como un levanta-pesas,
de las notas que ofrece: del "Daily Mirror", del "Times";
un guiño satisfecho, contaminado de medias mentiras.

Poner en orden las ideas, desoír esa persistente voz,
durante estas mañanas que anuncian las fiestas,
es una prueba de autoexigencia, de rechazo de ideas
impuestas: como tomar mate, jugar fútbol,
delirar por el tango o el rock, inclinarnos
ante la insistente mención de Irigoyen o Perón.

ENCOUNTER WITH THE VOICE

For Christmas I recount my years,
dark moments set in the bones.
Standing vigilant on the platform, buying a ticket,
entering and leaving through turnstiles,
being dragged along a canal of voices
to no particular destination.

Sheltered within the station's vaulted hall
my sliding body seeks a point,
a refuge of silence and minimal reflection
where all ill feelings examine themselves.
It finds its pathway strewn with tired thoughts
set deep in tired faces.

With neither organ nor Bible, alone with my wife,
the bed, bedside table, the middle of the night,
a dying lamp casting a weak glow, my room is no place
for my interior voice,
while she explores my moments,
shyly surmounting my shortcomings.

In the morning, with a half-open eye
on the cloudy sky, I stir the coffee,
chew the croissants, quickly flick through *Clarín*,
sighing as its writers strut their stuff like weightlifters,
"from *The Times*" or "the *Daily Mirror*" namedropped on every page
with a smug wink contaminated by half-truths and lies.

To block out that persistent voice and collect my thoughts
throughout mornings when the mind cries out for a holiday,
is a test of self-exigency, of my rejection of values that have been
drummed into us: like drinking maté, playing football,
raving over tango or rock, or the way we bend our ears
to the ubiquitous mentions of Irigoyen or Perón.

A las 7, (para "La Nación": seven o'clock),
entro en el bar, busco en su pequeña tiniebla
el rostro de un amigo. Dulce es el sueño
que trae una buena conversación, una antigua amistad,
lejos de los bares que rodean al Obelisco
(para "Clarín": nuestra "Trafalgar Square").

At 7 (or as *La Nación* would put it: "seven o'clock")
I enter the bar, peer through the smoky twilight
to find a friendly face. Sweet is the dream
brought by a good conversation, an old friendship,
far from the tourist-trap bars around the Obelisk
(for *Clarín*, our "Trafalgar Square").

TRUCOS DE LA VOZ INTERIOR

Aparto de mí, la trucada voz interior.
Por los destellos de la lámpara
evoco el recuerdo del bar,
lluvia sacudiendo los cristales,
y el deseo en aquella mujer
sincera, contundente, que me habla excitada
sin importarle su marido.

El deseo deambula en la charla,
lucha como un ser ciego
golpeándose codos, lengua, energías
en un galpón oscuro: mi ética,
donde la luz, el fuego
no asoman.

Ella pidió y yo también,
durante el murmullo de nuestras confesiones,
un instante para la ansiedad.
Fue un momento trágico, duro.
La conciencia no atiende estas súplicas.
Su brillante pero cenagosa corriente
sobre lo mejor, lo más vivo
de uno,
realiza masacres.

DECEITS OF THE INTERIOR VOICE

I free myself from the deceitful interior voice.
The glittering lamp takes me back
to that night in the bar,
the glasses tinkling beneath the rain,
and the desire of that woman,
frank and unabashed, the excitement
in her voice as she spoke to me
her husband far from her mind.

Desire pervades our conversation,
thrashes like a blind being,
flailing elbows, tongue and energies
in the darkened shack of my morality:
a dim, cold place
where all the lights have gone out.

Desperation crept into our voices
as we whispered our confessions,
all our fears revealed in an instant.
It was a tragic, unbearable moment.
Conscience does not listen to such entreaties.
Its brilliant but marsh-like flow
over all that is best, most living
in every one of us,
gives birth to massacres.

PRECIPICE IN THE SOUTH
DERRUMBE EN EL SUR

UN EXTENSO PAÍS

Un extenso país es una gran casa,
cada rincón contiene a la muerte,
pero no su aceleración. Muerte para
la liebre intrépida, para el escarabajo
por la lechuza, sequía en el arroyo.
Pausadamente la gran casa se traga
algunos hilos de la vida,
mide los silencios, no liquida el lenguaje.
Si el viento furioso agita sus cimientos
la casa enloquece, el lenguaje enloquece,
la muerte enloquece.
Cada día se vuelve el cumpleaños de la muerte,
nuestros nombres se hacen epitafios.

La propia casa es un lugar para morir
(después de una existencia activa),
soportando la llovizna y el frío
las mentiras acumuladas que nos
educaron. Sí, lo acepto,
la propia casa es un lugar
para vivir y morir,
si fuimos críticos con nuestra opinión
nacida del engaño,
y quebrada por nuestra duda.

A VAST COUNTRY

A vast country is a large house:
every corner contains death,
but lacks its hastening. Death for
the intrepid hare, for the beetle murdered
by the owl, the river by drought.
Slowly the large house swallows up
a few threads of life, measures the silences,
leaves the language intact.
When its foundations are shaken by furious winds
the house is deranged, language is deranged,
death is deranged.
Every day becomes death's birthday,
our names chiselled into epitaphs.

A person's house is a place in which to die
(after an active existence),
enduring the drizzle and the cold
and the accumulated lies
that formed our education. Yes, I agree,
a person's house is a place
in which to live and die,
if we are critics with our opinions
born of deceit
and broken by our doubts.

LA LAVANDERA MAPUCHE

El es ella debajo de mi ventana.
Por ese cuadrado gris el olor a bosta entra,
mezclado con la humedad de la ropa tendida
entre su voz de india y joven rockera,
y el polvillo de los eucaliptos
navegando en el viento.

Lava con el ritmo del agua en las cañerías,
recorriendo la casa como mis riñones
que descargo en la mañana,
oyendo algún pájaro o a ella cloqueando,
para llamar a las gallinas.

De cómo Zarza toma esta apariencia
intento atribuirlo al sueño o al malhumor.
El cielo muestra puntos negros,
De las piedras se eleva un polvillo de tormenta.

¿Qué me enceguece para no ver
que ella no mueve los labios,
que ocupa su mente en sacudirme,
al avanzar esta mañana de cambios
sobre la casa sola en el campo?

THE MAPUCHE WASHERGIRL

He is this girl below my window.
The smell of dung comes drifting in
through that grey square, mixed with the dampness
of the washing hung out to dry and the sound
of her young Indian rock-star voice,
while the fine dust of the eucalypti
sails on the wind.

She washes with the same rhythm as the water
that runs through the house's plumbing, and through
my kidneys when I relieve myself in the morning,
hearing a bird's song or her clucking
as she calls the chickens.

How does Zarza assume this appearance?
Am I dreaming? Is my mind playing tricks?
Black clouds are gathering in the sky,
a light dust-storm rises up from the stones.

> How could I be so blind as to not notice
> that she does not move her lips,
> her mind set solely on disturbing my peace,
> on advancing, this volatile morning,
> upon this solitary house in the country?

ANTE EL IMPOSTOR

Para el petulante poeta que fingía
por radio, ella sólo dedicó su lavado.
Fregó y fregó, sin inquietarse,
hecha una rana piadosa
susurrando su blues bajo el sauce.

Envuelto en la gran tormenta de sus mentiras,
semejante a la que amenazaba la casa,
este hombre mostró sus efectos.
En su voz había una aureola
de rayos y truenos, inequívocos sofismas.

Con el rostro mojado, ella-Zarza,
no detuvo su canto. La lluvia
dañó su ropa, pero no interrumpió
la radio. El agua sucia incesante
no la desilusionó.

Al relavar, concentrada en la soga,
con los sauces de frente y la radio distante,
ella se preguntó: ¿dónde leí
que una gran obra-tormenta
se disuelve en una lluvia de barro?

IN THE PRESENCE OF THE IMPOSTOR

To no one else but the self-satisfied
poet play-acting on the radio
did she dedicate her washing.
She scrubbed and scrubbed, her mind free of worries,
becoming more and more like a pious frog
murmuring its blues beneath the willow.

Trapped in the great storm of his lies
like the one that threatened to destroy the house,
the poet showed his affectations,
his voice crowned with a halo
of thunder and lightning, outrageous sophisms.

With her face wet, she-Zarza
went on singing regardless. The rain
ruined her clothes but still the radio
played on. The relentless filthy water
could not dampen her mood.

While busy with the second wash,
her eyes fixed on the clothesline,
facing the willows and with the radio out of earshot,
she wondered: Where was it that I read
that a great storm-work would be dissolved
in a rain of mud?

ESPIANDO A LOS ESCOLARES

Mirándolos a través de la ventana,
hermano y hermana, preocupados escolares,
borronean sus cuadernos, él se enoja,
discute y repite cómo
juega x con y, qué papel le otorgamos,
cuál es más y cuál menos.

Esos cerebritos pequeños, desde temprano,
injertados a una lógica rudimentaria,
no podrán cruzar al amplio mundo.
Desde el atardecer los veo
cerrar los puños, tensar las mandíbulas,
discutir lo irrazonable de x e y.

Y puede ser la nieve y x el refugio,
como x puede ser el mendigo
e y el plato de sopa. Pero
nunca x puede ser la navaja, e y
el esófago abierto. Sin embargo,
a través de la ventana,
los dos escolares
están luchando con este sinsentido.

OBSERVING THE SCHOOLCHILDREN

I watch them through the window,
brother and sister, two worried little scholars,
scribbling and crossing things out in their notebooks.
The brother gets annoyed, arguing over and over again
how x acts with y, what role we accord it,
which is more and which is less.

Those tiny little brains, grafted, at an early age,
on to a rudimentary logic,
will never find their way in the big wide world.
From late afternoon I watch
as they clench their fists, tense their jaws,
and discuss the irrationality of x and y.

Y can be the snow and x the shelter,
as x can be the beggar
and y the bowl of soup. But
never can x be the switchblade, nor y
the open oesophagus. Nevertheless,
through the open window,
the two schoolchildren
carry on struggling with this senselessness.

LA GRANJA-COMUNIDAD

El sol se asoma sobre el Puelo.
El poco pan, el guiso, el té
calientan, bailan en esos quince estómagos.
Y luego salen a reparar la cabaña
cosechar el maíz, leer en comunidad,
explicar uno por uno,
caída la noche
los lados oscuros de sus anteriores vidas.

Al resonar en la cabaña, de tablas crujientes,
dos o tres armónicas,
junto a las palmas, acompañando,
la cabaña ilumina al grupo
al peso de la nieve,
del grito sereno-pesado del invierno.

Llega septiembre y trae flores rojas
pero también trae lo otro,
psiquiatras, persecuciones, encierros,
para hacer de Zarza un muerto.

En la ambulancia, yendo al manicomio,
Zarza tuvo un sueño;
vió que Sigmund despertaba
y hallaba su Escuela como Catedral
y a sus discípulos como cardenales.
Bendecían y daban la extremaunción,
también consagraban bodas,
esta vez
entre el castigo y el silencio.

THE FARM-COMMUNITY

The sun comes up above the Puelo.
The meagre bread, the stew and the tea
give warmth and life to those fifteen stomachs.
And then they go out to repair the hut,
harvest the maize, enjoy a communal reading,
and recount one by one
when night has fallen
the dark sides of their former lives.

When filled with the sounds of harmonicas,
clapping hands and the floorboards creaking
beneath the stamping, dancing feet,
the hut lights up the group
despite the snow and the serene-
heavy cry of winter.

September arrives bringing red flowers,
but it also brings the other things:
psychiatrists, persecutions, imprisonments,
all aimed at turning Zarza into a dead man.

In the ambulance, going to the mental hospital,
Zarza had a dream:
he dreamt that Sigmund awoke
and found his School had turned into a Cathedral,
his disciples become cardinals.
They blessed and gave extreme unction,
consecrated marriages,
but this time
between punishment and silence.

CARTA DESDE EL MANICOMIO

Quiso escribir pero no pudo.
Deslizar, garabatear su recuerdo,
voces de infancia,
tratando, tratando,
pero no pudo.
Su sueño era pesado como el canal,
la acequia, con agua mansa
que le cubría el cuello,
le llenaba de globitos, helechos,
los ojos.
Trató, exigiéndole a sus dedos,
de escribir mi nombre, pero ellos
secta iracunda
no respondieron.
Fue cayendo, cayendo, hasta despertar,
y su despertar fue como su sueño:
ojos invertidos, pulpa de brisa,
desencajada y gritando ante un espejo.

LETTER FROM THE MENTAL HOSPITAL

He wanted to write but he couldn't.
To pour out, scrawl his memory,
all the voices of childhood;
he kept on trying, kept trying,
but he just couldn't do it.
His sleep was as heavy as the canal,
the irrigation ditch, its calm water
reaching up to his neck,
filling his eyes
with bubbles and pondweed.
He forced himself to have
one last try, ordering his fingers
to write my name, but like
an irascible sect
they were beyond response.
He was falling, falling, until waking up,
but when he woke up he was still asleep:
eyes turned inward, brain full of breeze,
contorted, screaming before a mirror.

DE PRONTO RECIBIMOS UNA CONSCIENCIA

De pronto recibimos una conciencia
rústicas camisas sin usar,
un saco de lana estrecho
telas de un muerto para
cubrir el cuerpo, y las llevamos,
y nos confiamos a esta herencia,
una variada memoria que va con nosotros.

En un armario se anuncian los viejos zapatos
junto a unos libros dispersos
cuelgan las corbatas como filamentos,
algas rarísimas, observando nuestro
silencio. La máquina de afeitar
abierta, como extraño coleóptero,
un maletín y los "Pensamientos" de Pascal,
una foto del muerto cuando tenía 30.

Sus objetos son su lengua
que tose en nuestros pensamientos,
irradian imágenes imposible de olvidar:
un ulular hiriente de ambulancia,
el goteo interminable del suero
la cama pulcra, el olor del sanatorio;
imágenes que nos forman.

Desde el centro de su visión
los muertos, unidos a la profunda tierra,
vienen hasta nosotros los vivos
y modelan nuestra memoria,
miran por nuestros ojos, se manifiestan
por nuestra lengua, dejan entre
ellos y nosotros, síntesis inconfundibles:
camisas, sueños, libros.

ALL AT ONCE WE RECEIVE ANOTHER'S CONSCIOUSNESS

All at once we receive another's consciousness:
unworn rustic shirts,
a tight-fitting jacket,
a dead man's objects
used for covering the body.
And we take them, we trust
in this inheritance,
a thousand memories to keep us company.

In a wardrobe are a collection of old shoes
and scattered books,
neckties hanging like filaments, weird algae,
calmly observing our silence. The electric shaver open
like a strange coleoptera,
a suitcase and the *Pensées* of Pascal,
a photograph of the dead man when he was 30 years old.

His objects are his tongue
coughing in our thoughts,
evoking images impossible to forget:
the piercing scream of the ambulance,
the relentless drip-drip of serum,
the antiseptically clean bed, the sanatorium smell;
images that make us what we are.

From the centre of his vision
the dead, united in the deep soil,
come towards us the living
and shape our memory,
see through our eyes, manifest themselves
through our tongue, filling the space
between the dead and the living
with unmistakable combinations:
shirts
dreams
books.

AFTER DEATH, I BEGIN AGAIN
DESPUÉS DE LA MUERTE, RECOMIENZO

DESPUÉS DE LA MUERTE, RECOMIENZO

Emergiendo del agua lo cubrió una luz.
En infinitos segundos Zarza fue
todos los rostros de la región:
el chico que recogía bosta del ganado,
la que cantaba lavando la ropa,
el rabino o el cura metidos en
sus libros, el asesino y sus ojos alucinantes,
el hospicio, la navaja, el televisor,
una delgada franja de bruma sobre el lago.
Cuando me aproximé a él, era roca,
brutal peñasco que ofrecía su lágrima.
Así renació por un momento.

Luego se fue, como pareja de novios.

AFTER DEATH, I BEGIN AGAIN

As he emerged from the water he was bathed in light.
In infinite seconds Zarza assumed
the appearance of every person
and thing for miles around:
the boy who collected cow dung for a living,
the girl who sang while washing clothes,
the rabbi or priest absorbed in
their books, the murderer with his dazzling eyes,
the hostel, the switchblade, the television,
a thin layer of mist above the lake.
When I approached him he was a rock,
a rough crag displaying a single wet tear.
And thus, for one moment, he was reborn.

And then he left, as a couple of newly-weds.

PARA TERMINAR CON LA PAREJA

Frenéticos, jadeantes, suben la colina
bajan exhaustos, se friegan las manos,
comen cortezas de pan.

No más de veinte años, hombre y mujer,
pareja que se desprendió de un riñón
de Zarza.

Y la vida canta por ellos, aún
deambulando entre piedras.

Y la armónica de él repite una
melodía de Bach, con croar de aviones
sobre sus cabezas.

Después del río, llega la noche.
Son espiados por ojos de tanques.

En la noche del campo reina la armónica,
pero un estruendo de misil
disuelve esta apariencia.

Zarza vuelve a lo que fue:
rey de huesos dispersos.

TO BE DONE WITH THE COUPLE

Mad with joy, panting, they run up the hill,
then run back down exhausted,
rub their hands, eat crusts of bread.

No more than twenty years old,
Man and Woman,
the couple born from the kidney
of Zarza.

And life sings for them
as they stroll among the rocks.

And his harmonica keeps on playing
a Bach melody, accompanied by the croaking
of aeroplanes flying above their heads.

They reach the bank of the river and the night comes down.
The eyes of tanks have them in their sights.

At night in the country the harmonica reigns,
but a missile explosion
dissolves this illusion.

Zarza turns back into his real self:
the king of scattered bones.

LA TELEVISIÓN MULTIPLICA SIEMPRE

La voz lo sobresaltó, copiaba su sombra,
llenaba la pantalla.
Incrédulo la escuchó conmover,
girando con sus mismas muecas.
"Confíen en mí", mintió
en cada bar, en cada sala somnolienta
de cada pueblito.

Zarza estaba multiplicado. Con una voz
en falsete, auguraba o maldecía
en las colinas, en los dormitorios,
aserraderos, despachos,
o el discreto barcito del lujoso
hotel.

Crecía, se agolpaba, quería ser
una palabra digna.

Pero el comercio pudo más.

Zarza respiró.

Pero el Poder pudo más.

Zarza respiró.

Los noticieros desplazaron la imagen de su doble
muy lejos.

La mentira –pensó Zarza–
muere tapada por mentiras gigantes.

TELEVISION MULTIPLYING INTO INFINITY

The voice made him jump –
he saw a copy of his own shadow
filling the TV screen.
Incredulous he heard its winning spiel,
every expression on its face
mirroring his own.
"Trust in me," it lied
in every bar, every dormitory,
in every tiny little town.

Zarza was multiplying. With a falsetto
voice, he spat predictions and curses
in the hills, in the bedrooms,
in sawmills and offices,
or in the luxury hotel's
discreet little bar.

He grew, he thronged, strove to become
a worthy word.

But commerce could do more.

(Zarza breathed in)

But Power could do more.

(Zarza breathed in)

News programmes shifted his double's image
far far away.

The lie – thought Zarza –
dies stifled by gigantic lies.

BAR "TRELEW"

¿Yatasto? Yatasto era el mejor,
pero considere Ud. a Forli
era insuperable, como Gardel;
yo no lo diría así
¿nunca fue Ud. conmovido
por Julio Sosa?
Vamos, vamos, yo le hablo de canto
no de cantitos de chingolos;
le molestaría a Ud. pedirme otra cerveza,
de ninguna manera, Ud. se lo merece,
pero yo agregaría que en cuanto a tono
no leí nada igual a Banchs;
lo siento mi amigo, pero reparó
en la voz elegante de Girri?
por favor, señor, es tan elegante
como una pata de cerdo,
no, no, vea Ud. esa cadencia,
¿cadencia? ¡las pelotas! y disculpe
pero para leerlo hay que ponerse smoking...

Amables, los graduados en
El Salvador y Trinity College,
Baires y Eton se hundieron

en la oscuridad que Zarza
(el Fugaz reemplazante del cantinero)
al cerrar, produjo.

Invisible, se entregó a la noche
a todas sus abigarradas voces,
al eco de las risueñas, pícaras
voces de los graduados,
o de las melodías que le dejó la radio
de "La Rosa púrpura de El Cairo",

"TRELEW" BAR

Yatasto? Yes, Yatasto was the greatest,
but don't forget Forli –
no one could beat him, the same with Gardel
I wouldn't put it that way –
have you never been moved
by Julio Sosa's voice?
Aw, come on, I'm talking about *singing*,
not the tweetings of a chingolo;
could I trouble you for another beer?
no trouble at all, you more than deserve it,
but I would add as far as harmony's concerned
that I've never read anything that bears comparison with Banchs
well I'm sorry, my friend, but aren't you forgetting
the elegant voice of Girri?
oh please, sir! I've seen more elegance
in a pig's backside,
no, no, just look at this rhythm,
you call *that* rhythm? bollocks!
I'm sorry but you have to
wear a tuxedo just to read it…

These amiable undergraduates
of El Salvador and Trinity College,
Baires and Eton slowly sink

into the darkness that Zarza
(the Fleeting One who has taken the barman's place)
produced as a finale.

Invisible, he gave himself to the night
with all its sundry voices,
the echoing laughter of the girls,
the undergraduates' crude remarks,
or the radio playing melodies
from *The Purple Rose of Cairo*,

acariciando despacio su dolor
con la voz de la señorita Piggy
acompañada por la rana René;
voces suaves y armoniosas,
antes de entrar en el agua
para transformarse en el Chubut
que nos despertaría a las 4.30,
profundo y jocoso
como una cancioncita de los Muppets.

slowly soothing his pain
with the voice of Miss Piggy
accompanied by Kermit The Frog;
soft, harmonious voices fading out
as he steps into the water
then re-emerges transformed into The Chubut,
which wakes us up at 4.30,
profound and comic
like a little song from The Muppets.

EL CHUBUT DEJA SU HISTORIA DE LA AMISTAD

Los ojos encendidos, las lenguas trabadas,
los dos viejos amigos de amenazan.

Cuando el puño de uno
va a caer sobre el rostro del otro,
viene el policía, habla con los dos
y me mira.

"Yo le dí doscientos dólares
me trajo el cambio de cien,
se guardó el otro billete".

"Me dió un billete falso.
Le devolví su vieja trampa".

El policía se inclina y me dice:
"¿declara como testigo señor?"
Todo el bar espera mi respuesta.

"Entre dos tramposos no sé cuál elegir".

De pronto ante mi asombro
el policía se transforma en crítico literario:
"¿sería jurado del concurso de poesía
de la Fundación S.A.?"

"¿A quién debo elegir, señor?"

No conforme,
con cara y atuendo de obispo,
me sermonea:
"Estás tentado por Dios y el Diablo".

"Los dos me están corrompiendo", le confieso.

THE CHUBUT BEQUEATHS ITS HISTORY OF FRIENDSHIP

Eyes blazing, tongues tied,
the two old friends exchange threats.

Just as the fist of one is about to connect
with the face of the other
a policeman turns up, asks what's going on
and throws the odd glance in my direction.

"I gave him two hundred dollars
and he gave me change for one hundred –
he kept the rest for himself."

"He gave me a counterfeit banknote –
it was an old trick and I paid him back for it."

The policeman leans over and says to me:
"Would you provide a witness statement sir?"
The whole bar falls quiet as they await my answer.

"Between two deceivers I don't know which one to choose."

Suddenly, to my astonishment,
the policeman turns into a literary critic:
"Would you be a juror for the Foundation
Ltd's poetry competition?"

"Which one should I choose, sir?"

Not satisfied with this answer,
and wearing a bishop's face and garb,
he lectures me:
"You are tempted by God and the Devil."

"The two are corrupting me," I confess.

Pero, el último, el cocinero
robusto y blanco como la nieve
dice con la voz del policía:
"para la cena que elige: ¿pato o gallareta?"

"gallipato", carraspeo.

"No señor", me dice colérico el policía,
"lo suyo es tramposo";

levanto mi abrigo, pago mi vino
y le respondo:
"Tramposa es la elección"

"¿co-co-cómo?"

"Sí. Quienes más nos aman,
más nos engañan".

But then the cook, the last in line,
robust and white as snow,
asks with the policeman's voice:
"What will you have for dinner: duck or coot?"

"Cootduck," I reply,
clearing my throat.

"No sir," says the policeman angrily,
"you are being deceitful";

I pick up my coat, pay for my wine
and answer him:
"It is the choice that is deceitful;

"W-w-what?"

"Yes. They who love us most
deceive us most."

PARA LA MEMORIA NO HAY OLVIDO

Para la memoria no hay olvido
ella trabaja a pesar nuestro,
de engañosos hábitos o viejas perversiones,
es imposible ocultar
lo que eternamente vuelve.

Pudimos hacer, pero no lo hicimos,
es irreversible,
se lo tragó el tiempo.
Pero aún podemos hacer,
cambiar, darnos algún sentido.

El mar barriendo,
lo que en la playa se construye,
tiene semejanza con nuestro recuerdo.

Allí estamos indiferentes,
rutinarios, yendo y viniendo,
mecánicos como el oleaje,
instalados en una repetición perpetua
un movimiento que nos hace inmutables.

Ese tal vez sea el aspecto
que más nos horroriza del mar,
tragarlo todo, una y otra vez,
por millones de años,
sin memoria.

FOR MEMORY THERE IS NO OBLIVION

For memory there is no oblivion,
nothing fades no matter
how hard we try.
Of our deceitful customs and old perversions,
it is impossible to hide
that which eternally returns.

We could have acted but we did not act;
now the moment is irreversible,
time swallowed it up.
But we can still act,
change, give ourselves some meaning.

The sea that sweeps away
everything built on the beach
echoes the workings of our memory.

For we are thoughtless
creatures of habit bustling back and forth,
as mechanical as the ebb and flow of the sea –
stuck in an unending repetition,
a movement that renders us immutable.

It is perhaps this that most horrifies
us about the sea,
the way it swallows everything, again and again,
over millions of years,
without memory.

ANTES DE UNIRNOS, EN GAIMAN

Antes de unirnos, en Gaiman
recibo tu voz, espeso follaje,
junto a mi cama (diarios de por medio)
dulce y árida mujer que comenta:
cáncer del presidente hemipléjico, próstata
del líder fundamentalista, nube mortífera,
crímenes rituales, las dos capillas galesas
ocultas, resplandecientes.

Pero luego desechás los diarios.
Dos filosas piedras en mi cráneo
son tus ojos. Te quejás, gritás, contra
ese lameculos y obstinado escritor
hijo de una raza de chupaculos,
al tiempo que me llamás:
"pedagogo-boludo".

La alfalfa nocturna recorrida por el viento
nos distrae, te vuelve más áspera.
En verano el campo luce inquieto, estrecho.
Un encierro, donde las ilusiones
son eludidas por tu dolor,
comentadas por tus ojos,
y el amor, es aquel remoto sauce
confundido con otros árboles.

BEFORE WE COME TOGETHER, IN GAIMAN

Before we come together, in Gaiman
I hear your voice, dense verbiage,
at the side of my bed (a mess of newspapers)
a sweet, dry woman with plenty to say
about the hemiplegic president's cancer, the fundamentalist
leader's prostate, a poison-gas cloud,
ritual crimes, the two hidden
resplendent Welsh chapels.

But then you'll throw the newspapers to one side.
Your eyes are two sharp stones
boring into my skull. You will complain, launch invectives
against a certain persistent, arse-licking writer,
son of a race of slimy arse-kissers;
and at the same time you will call me
"bollock-brain pedagogue".

The nocturnal alfalfa rustling in the wind
distracts us, and you become even harsher.
The countryside in summer has a restless, restricted air.
An enclosure in which hopes
are avoided by your sorrow,
remarked upon by your eyes;
and love is that distant willow
lost among the other trees.

ES LA EXTRAÑA NOCHE QUE NOS DESNUDA

Es la extraña noche que nos desnuda
en la hora más quieta,
sólo el viento habla en la calle
los árboles y las sombras conservan su letargo
y la sustancia de nuestra fe cruje,
rápida se vuelve autocompasión,
los fracasos acumulados se quieren disimular
no hay otro mérito que exhibir equilibrio,
son unas horas amargas, implacables,
sólo preocupadas en mostrar cómo somos.

Admitir que lo que uno puso afuera
(Zarza), es lo que uno tuvo adentro,
es admitir cómo
nuestra madurez retoca nuestra juventud,
como nuestros sueños rehacen la desdicha.
Así vemos a nuestra mujer
moldeada por nuestras ideas.
Ellas pulen todo lo imperfecto,
pero lo perfecto es nuestro tormento,
en cambio,
nuestras derrotas son nuestra liberación.

Sí, la noche y la calle desierta
vienen a mostrar
el dolor de todo vacío,
el momento más oscuro, mezclado
con la claridad. Nuestro orgasmo
con la falsificación de su recuerdo.
Admitir esta combinación es
trabajo entre sueños,
la penosa vigilia
donde nos redimen nuestros errores,
no nuestros aciertos.

IT IS THE STRANGE NIGHT THAT UNDRESSES US

It is the strange night that undresses us
in the calmest hour,
when the wind is the only voice in the street,
the trees and shadows are frozen in lethargy
and the substance of our faith begins to creak,
quickly becoming self-pity.
All the failures and humiliations of a lifetime
try in vain to hide themselves.
The only thing you can hope for is to *appear* sane.
They are bitter hours, implacable,
concerned only with showing us how we are.

To admit that the person you are on the outside
(Zarza) is no different from what you are inside
is to admit how
our maturity retouches our youth,
as our dreams reverse all misfortunes.
And so we see our lover
as moulded by our ideas.
They polish all that is imperfect,
and yet the perfect is that which
truly tortures us,
while our defeats are our liberation.

Yes, the night and the deserted street
come to show us
the pain of all emptiness,
the darkest moment infused
with clarity. Our orgasm
with our false memory of it.
To admit this combination
is our task between dreams,
the laborious vigil
where we redeem our errors,
not our successes.

BIOGRAPHICAL NOTES

FERNANDO KOFMAN was born in the Argentine province of Misiones in 1947, and has lived in Buenos Aires since the late 1960s. He has had seven books of poetry published in his own country, including *Zarza remueve* and *Tres óperas politicas*, as well as books of essays. In addition to editing a volume of minimalist North American poetry, he has been involved with the magazines *Batataria* and *Satura* and in 2005 founded *FrankBaires (La escuela de Frankfurt en Buenos Aires)*, a journal intended to show the links between philosophy, poetry and politics in the contemporary world.

IAN TAYLOR was born in Liverpool in 1967, spent his childhood in the small Lancashire town of Ince and has spent the last decade living in the small-ish North Dorset village of Thornford. His own writings – poetry, prose and reviews – have appeared in various magazines in the UK, US and Argentina, while his first poetry collection, *Ruins*, was published by Spectacular Diseases in 1997. Between 1997 and 2001 he edited the avant-garde small-press magazine *écorché*. His first novel, based on an experience of homelessness in Buenos Aires, is currently seeking a publisher. In addition to *Zarza remueve*, he has also translated Kofman's *De Bell a Campana* and *La cultura depende del lenguaje*.

ANDREW GRAHAM-YOOLL was born in 1944 in Buenos Aires of a Scottish father and an English mother. He is the author of about twenty books, in English and in Spanish. He was the editor of the English-language *Buenos Aires Herald* (founded in 1876) up to December 2007, having joined the paper in 1966. In 1976, he left the *Herald* and went into exile during the military dictatorship, but in 1994 he returned to Argentina where he became editor and president of the board of the *Herald*.

Graham-Yooll's books include the now classic *A State of Fear: Memories of Argentina's Nightmare* (1985), which author Graham Greene called "the book of the year" at the time. He is also known for *The Forgotten Colony: A History of the English-speaking Communities in Argentina*, first published in 1981.

He translates Spanish poetry into English, and British and US poets into Spanish. In 2002, he was awarded the Order of the

British Empire (OBE), by the British Crown. He has four children and three grandchildren.

Also available in the Arc Publications
'VISIBLE POETS' SERIES
(Series Editor: Jean Boase-Beier)

No. 1
MIKLÓS RADNÓTI (Hungary)
Camp Notebook
TRANSLATED BY FRANCIS JONES
INTRODUCED BY GEORGE SZIRTES

No. 2
BARTOLO CATTAFI (Italy)
Anthracite
TRANSLATED BY BRIAN COLE
INTRODUCED BY PETER DALE
(Poetry Book Society Recommended Translation)

No. 3
MICHAEL STRUNGE (Denmark)
A Virgin from a Chilly Decade
TRANSLATED BY BENTE ELSWORTH
INTRODUCED BY JOHN FLETCHER

No. 4
TADEUSZ RÓZEWICZ (Poland)
recycling
TRANSLATED BY BARBARA BOGOCZEK (PLEBANEK) & TONY HOWARD
INTRODUCED BY ADAM CZERNIAWSKI

No. 5
CLAUDE DE BURINE (France)
Words Have Frozen Over
TRANSLATED BY MARTIN SORRELL
INTRODUCED BY SUSAN WICKS

No. 6
CEVAT ÇAPAN (Turkey)
Where Are You, Susie Petschek?
TRANSLATED BY CEVAT ÇAPAN & MICHAEL HULSE
INTRODUCED BY A. S. BYATT

No. 7
JEAN CASSOU (France)
33 Sonnets of the Resistance
WITH AN ORIGINAL INTRODUCTION BY LOUIS ARAGON
TRANSLATED BY TIMOTHY ADÈS
INTRODUCED BY ALISTAIR ELLIOT

No. 8
ARJEN DUINKER (Holland)
The Sublime Song of a Maybe
TRANSLATED BY WILLEM GROENEWEGEN
INTRODUCED BY JEFFREY WAINWRIGHT

No. 9
MILA HAUGOVÁ (Slovakia)
Scent of the Unseen
TRANSLATED BY JAMES & VIERA SUTHERLAND-SMITH
INTRODUCED BY FIONA SAMPSON

No. 10
ERNST MEISTER (Germany)
Between Nothing and Nothing
TRANSLATED BY JEAN BOASE-BEIER
INTRODUCED BY JOHN HARTLEY WILLIAMS

No. 11
YANNIS KONDOS (Greece)
Absurd Athlete
TRANSLATED BY DAVID CONNOLLY
INTRODUCED BY DAVID CONSTANTINE

No. 12
BEJAN MATUR (Turkey)
In the Temple of a Patient God
TRANSLATED BY RUTH CHRISTIE
INTRODUCED BY MAUREEN FREELY

No. 13
GABRIEL FERRATER (Catalonia / Spain)
Women and Days
TRANSLATED BY ARTHUR TERRY
INTRODUCED BY SEAMUS HEANEY

No. 14
INNA LISNIANSKAYA (Russia)
Far from Sodom
TRANSLATED BY DANIEL WEISSBORT
INTRODUCED BY ELAINE FEINSTEIN

No. 15
SABINE LANGE (Germany)
The Fishermen Sleep
TRANSLATED BY JENNY WILLIAMS
INTRODUCED BY MARY O'DONNELL

No. 16
TAKAHASHI MUTSUO (Japan)
We of Zipangu
TRANSLATED BY JAMES KIRKUP & TAMAKI MAKOTO
INTRODUCED BY GLYN PURSGLOVE

No. 17
JURIS KRONBERGS (Latvia)
Wolf One-Eye
TRANSLATED BY MARA ROZITIS
INTRODUCED BY JAAN KAPLINSKI

No. 18
REMCO CAMPERT (Holland)
I Dreamed in the Cities at Night
TRANSLATED BY DONALD GARDNER
INTRODUCED BY PAUL VINCENT

No. 19
DOROTHEA ROSA HERLIANY (Indonesia)
Kill the Radio
TRANSLATED BY HARRY AVELING
INTRODUCED BY LINDA FRANCE

No. 20
SOLEIMAN ADEL GUÉMAR (Algeria)
State of Emergency
TRANSLATED BY TOM CHEESMAN & JOHN GOODBY
INTRODUCED BY LISA APPIGNANESI

No. 21
ELI TOLARETXIPI (Basque)
Still Life with Loops
TRANSLATED BY PHILIP JENKINS
INTRODUCED BY ROBERT CRAWFORD